A Zooful of Animals

A Zooful

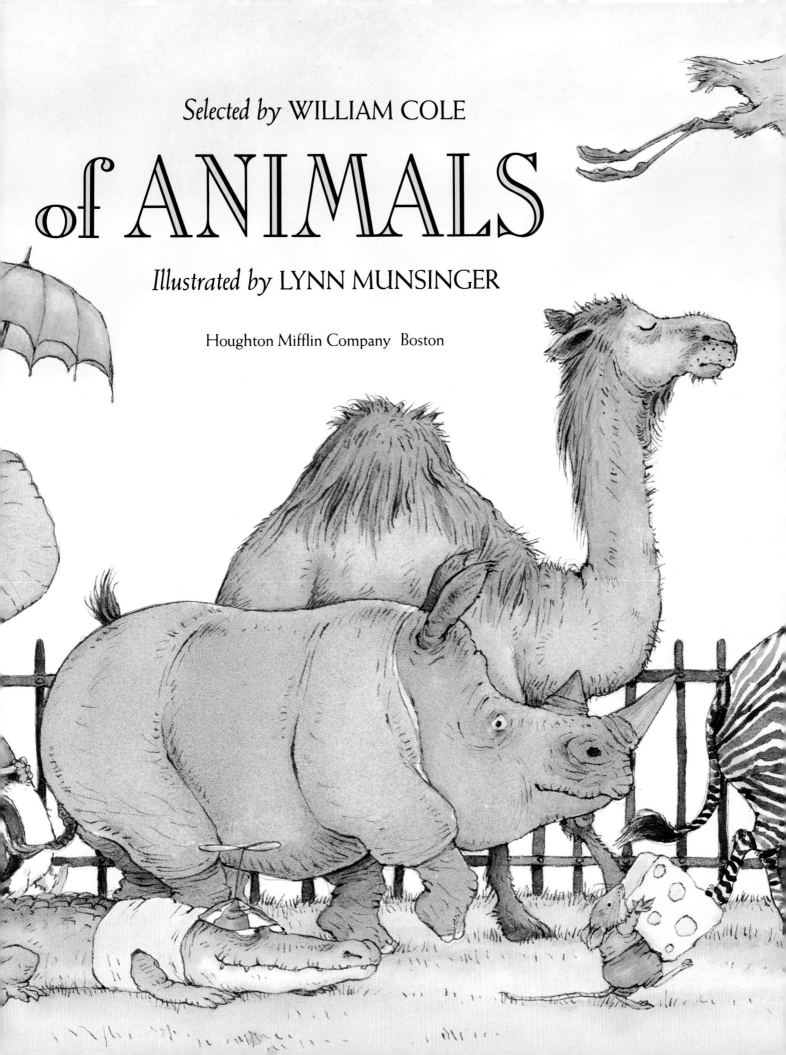

Selected by WILLIAM COLE

# of ANIMALS

Illustrated by LYNN MUNSINGER

Houghton Mifflin Company Boston

Library of Congress Cataloging-in-Publication Data

A Zooful of animals / selected by William Cole; illustrated by
Lynn Munsinger.

p. cm.

Includes index.

Summary: A collection of animal poems by authors including
Rachel Field, X. J. Kennedy, and John Ciardi.

ISBN 0-395-52278-1   PAP ISBN 0-395-77873-5

1. Animals—Juvenile poetry. 2. Children's poetry, American.
3. Children's poetry, English. [1. Animals—Poetry. 2. American
poetry—Collections. 3. English poetry—Collections.] I. Cole,
William, 1919–   II. Munsinger, Lynn, ill.

PS595.A5Z66 1992   91-21885

811.008'036—dc20   CIP   AC

For information about this and other Houghton Mifflin trade
and reference books and multimedia products, visit
The Bookstore at Houghton Mifflin on the World Wide Web
at http://www.hmco.com/trade/ .

Printed in the United States of America.
Copyright acknowledgments begin on page 87.
WOZ 10 9 8 7 6 5 4 3

CONTENTS

A Zooful of Animals

INTRODUCTION

My Zoo is open to all,
Even the horse in the stall,
Even the puppy and cat —
Even the mouse and the rat!
Leapers and flyers and creepers,
Honkers and roarers and peepers,
Fur or feathers or hide —
Everyone lives inside.
They all can be found in these pages.
My Zoo doesn't have any cages!

So come on, step into the Zoo —
The animals all welcome you!

William Cole

WOULDN'T IT BE FUNNY?

Now, wouldn't it be funny
If the creatures in the Zoo
Were all let out to walk about
And look at me and you?

And wouldn't it be funny
If they put us in the cages,
And Kangaroos and Cockatoos
Came guessing at our ages.

And wouldn't it be funny
If the Hip-po-pot-amus
Said, "Don't go near, I really fear
They're very dangerous."

Pixie O'Harris

THE TOUCAN

Of all the birds I know, few can
Boast of as large a bill as the toucan.
Yet I can think of one who can,
And if you think a while, too, you can:
Another toucan
In the zoo can.

Pyke Johnson, Jr.

14

PYGMY ELEPHANT

The Pygmy Elephant is made
Much shorter than the giant brigade.
He lives much closer to the ground
And that is where he's usually found.
Why should an Elephant be so wee?
My friend, it's no good asking *me!*

Spike Milligan

THE TIGER

A tiger going for a stroll
Met an old man and ate him whole.

The old man shouted, and he thumped,
The tiger's stomach churned and bumped.

The other tigers said: "Now really,
We hear your breakfast much too clearly."

The moral is, he should have chewed.
It does no good to bolt one's food.

Edward Lucie-Smith

THE ELEPHANT

Of all the facts about mammals
This is most relevant:
It takes a lot of paper
To gift-wrap an elephant.

Louis Phillips

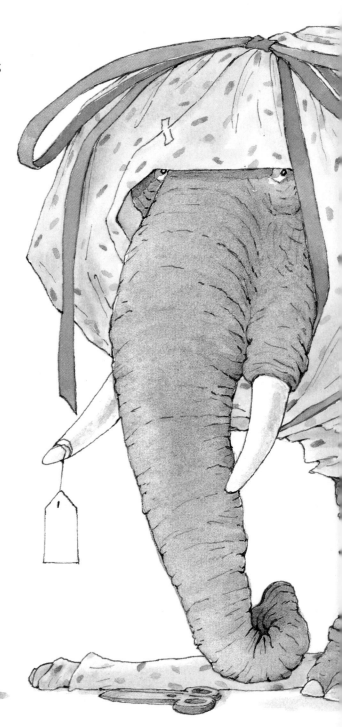

HOW TO TELL THE WILD ANIMALS

If ever you should go by chance
    To jungles in the East;
And if there should to you advance
    A large and tawny beast,
If he roars at you as you're dyin'
You'll know it is the Asian Lion.

Or if some time when roaming round,
    A noble wild beast greets you,
With black stripes on a yellow ground,
    Just notice if he eats you.
This simple rule may help you learn
The Bengal Tiger to discern.

If strolling forth, a beast you view,
　　Whose hide with spots is peppered,
As soon as he has lept on you,
　　You'll know it is the Leopard.
'Twill do no good to roar with pain,
He'll only lep and lep again.

If when you're walking round your yard,
　　You meet a creature there,
Who hugs you very, very hard,
　　Be sure it is the Bear.
If you have any doubt, I guess
He'll give you just one more caress.

Though to distinguish beasts of prey
    A novice might nonplus,
The Crocodiles you always may
    Tell from Hyenas thus:
Hyenas come with merry smiles;
But if they weep, they're Crocodiles.

The true Chameleon is small,
    A lizard sort of thing;
He hasn't any ears at all,
    And not a single wing.
If there is nothing in the tree,
'Tis the Chameleon you see.

Carolyn Wells

ABOUT THE TEETH OF SHARKS

The thing about a shark is — teeth,
One row above, one row beneath.

Now take a close look. Do you find
It has another row behind?

Still closer — here, I'll hold your hat:
Has it a third row behind that?

Now look in and . . . Look out! Oh my,
I'll never know now! Well, goodbye.

John Ciardi

JIM-JAM PYJAMAS

He wears striped jim-jam pyjamas,
You never saw jim-jams like those,
A fine-fitting, stretchy, fur cat-suit,
Skin-tight from his head to his toes.

He wears striped jim-jam pyjamas,
Black and yellow and dashingly gay;
He makes certain that everyone sees them
By keeping them on all the day.

He wears striped jim-jam pyjamas,
He walks with a smug-pussy stride;
There's no hiding his pride in his jim-jams
With their zig-zaggy lines down each side.

He wears striped jim-jam pyjamas
And pauses at times to display
The effect as he flexes his torso —
Then he fancies he hears people say:

"I wish I had jim-jam pyjamas!
I wish I were feline and slim!
Oh, look at that brave Bengal tiger!
Oh, how I should love to be him!"

Gina Wilson

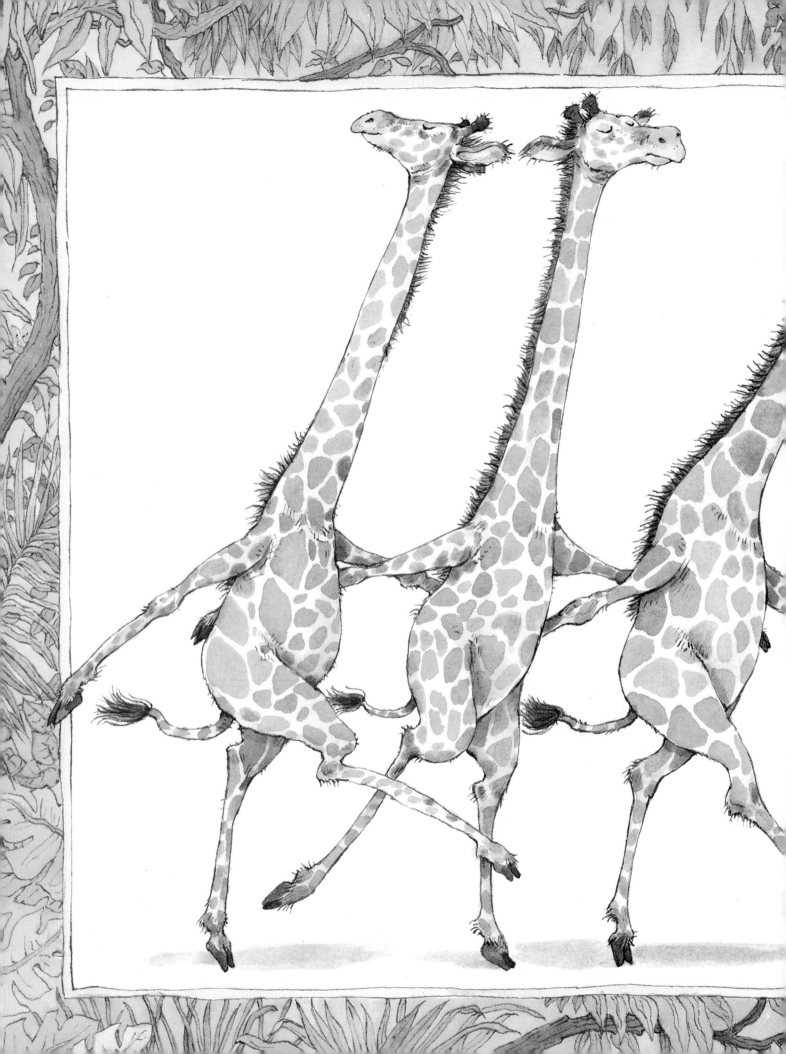

THE GIRAFFE

Hide of a leopard and hide of a deer
    And eyes of a baby calf,
Sombre and large and crystal-clear,
And a comical back that is almost sheer
    Has the absurd giraffe.

A crane all covered with hide and hair
    Is the aslant giraffe
So cleverly mottled with many a square
That even the jungle is unaware
Whether a pair or a herd is there,
    Or possibly one giraffe
    Or possibly only half.

If you saw him stoop and straddle and drink
    He would certainly make you laugh
He would certainly make you laugh, I think,
With his head right down on the water's brink,
    Would the invert giraffe,
The comical, knock-kneed, angular, crock-kneed,
    Anyhow-built giraffe.

There's more than a grain of common sense
        And a husky lot of chaff
In the many and various arguments
        About the first giraffe,
        The first and worst giraffe:
Whether he grew a neck because
        He yearned for the higher shoots
        Out of the reach of all and each
        Of the ruminating brutes;
Or whether he got to the shoots because
His neck was long, if long it was,
        Is the cause of many disputes:
Over the ladder without any rungs
The stopper-like mouth and the longest of tongues
        Of the rum and dumb giraffe,
        The How-did-you-come giraffe,
The brown equatorial, semi-arboreal
        Head-in-the-air giraffe.

Geoffrey Dearmer

SUPPER FOR A LION

Savage lion in the zoo,
Walking by on padded feet,
To and fro and fro and to,
You seem to think it's time to eat.

Then how about a bowl of stew
With Jell-O for dessert? Or would
A juicy bone be best for you?

Oh, please don't stare
    as though you knew
        That I'd taste good!

Dorothy Aldis

THE HYENA

The hyena is
A funny bloke,
He'll laugh at almost
Any joke,
So if you have
A joke that's dim,
Go and tell your joke
To him.

Mike Thaler

OLD MAN PLATYPUS

Far from the trouble and toil of town,
Where the reed-beds sweep and shiver,
Look at a fragment of velvet brown —
Old Man Platypus drifting down,
Drifting along the river.

And he plays and dives in the river bends
In a style that is most elusive;
With few relations and fewer friends,
For Old Man Platypus descends
From a family most exclusive.

He shares his burrow beneath the bank
With his wife and his son and daughter
At the roots of the reeds and the grasses rank;
And the bubbles show where our hero sank
To its entrance under water.

Safe in their burrow below the falls
They live in a world of wonder,
Where no one visits and no one calls,
They sleep like little brown billiard balls
With their beaks tucked neatly under.

And he talks in a deep unfriendly growl
As he goes on his journey lonely;
For he's no relation to fish nor fowl,
Nor to bird nor beast, nor to horned owl;
In fact, he's the one and only!

A. B. Paterson

IN PRAISE OF LLAMAS

La-la-llamas rate as mammals
Much resembling baby camels,
And their appellation's hard to speak and spell,
For it seems, when Adam uttered
Their baptismal name, he stuttered,
Hence we always must reduplicate the "L."

Those Peruvians, the Incas,
On their lonely mountain fincas
(Which is Spanish for plantations, ranches, farms)
Reared, instead of Leghorns, Brahmas
And Minorcas, La-la-llamas
With Alpacas who have corresponding charms.

Through Andean panoramas
Wind the herds of La-la-llamas,
Skirting precipices dangerously steep,
Over swinging bridge or ferry
To some La-la-llamaserai,
Or wherever La-la-llamas stop to sleep.

Lively lambkin La-la-llamas
Trot beside their ma-ma-ma-mas,
Lightly dancing when their parents pause to graze;
Lovely lady La-la-llamas
Look like queens of movie dramas
With their melting eyes and soft, coquettish ways.

And they splash across lagunas
With their cousins, the Vicunas
And Guanacos, bearing loads upon their backs;
And these useful La-la-llamas
Furnish wool to make pajamas
And to help their owners pay the income tax.

So be happy, La-la-llamas
Climbing Western Fujiyamas
Or descending to the vega's fertile floor!
Thrive and flourish, La-la-llamas,
In a clime like Alabama's,
In Bolivia, Peru and Ecuador!

Arthur Guiterman

ARE YOU A MARSUPIAL?

Now are you a marsupial?
And have you a little pouch?
If I pinch it on the outside
Does something inside holler "Ouch!"?

John Becker

CROCODILE OR ALLIGATOR?

Crocodile or alligator,
Who is who on the equator?
Which one ate up Auntie Norah,
Famous tropical explorer?

Cool she was and calm she kept, I'll
Bet you that repulsive reptile
Had a hard job as he ate her,
Crocodile *or* alligator.

Norah, sister of my mother,
Couldn't tell one from the other,
Had she only read this fable,
Maybe she'd have then been able.

Crocodiles, with jaws shut tightly,
Show their teeth off impolitely,
But alligators aren't so rude,
And seldom let their teeth protrude.

Whether former, whether latter,
To Aunt Norah doesn't matter,
She's at rest inside his tummy,
What a dinner, yummy, yummy!

Colin West

ANACONDA

A snake to fear
Is the anaconda —
He stretches from here

to over yonder.

Doug Macleod

THE BAT

By day the bat is cousin to the mouse.
He likes the attic of an aging house.

His fingers make a hat about his head.
His pulse beat is so slow we think him dead.

He loops in crazy figures half the night
Among the trees that face the corner light.

But when he brushes up against a screen,
We are afraid of what our eyes have seen:

For something is amiss or out of place
When mice with wings can wear a human face.

Theodore Roethke

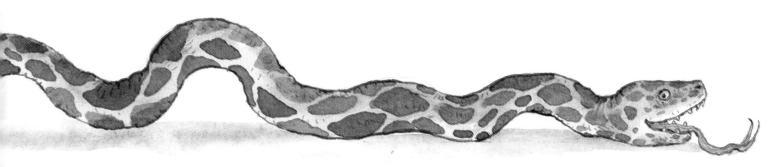

GROWING UP

Little Tommy Tadpole began to weep and wail,
For little Tommy Tadpole had lost his little tail,
And his mother didn't know him, as he wept upon a log;
For he wasn't Tommy Tadpole, but Mr. Thomas Frog.

C. J. Dennis

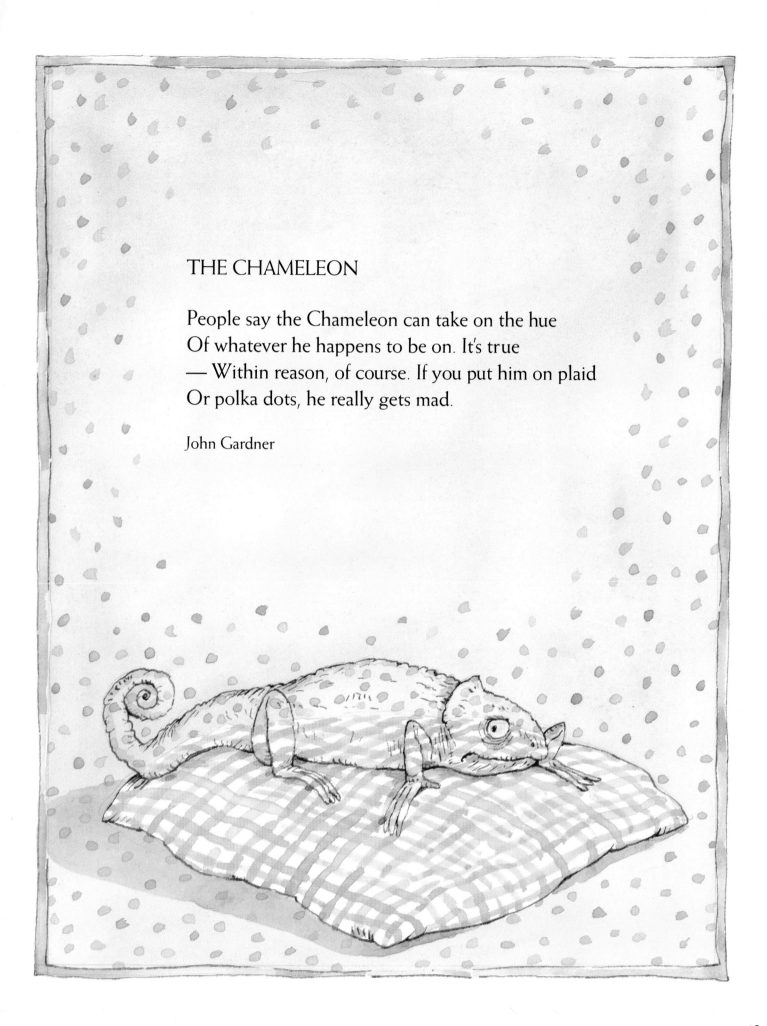

THE CHAMELEON

People say the Chameleon can take on the hue
Of whatever he happens to be on. It's true
— Within reason, of course. If you put him on plaid
Or polka dots, he really gets mad.

John Gardner

THE SONG OF MR. TOAD

The world has held great Heroes,
    As history books have showed;
But never a name to go down to fame
    Compared with that of Toad!

The clever men at Oxford
    Know all that there is to be knowed.
But they none of them knew one half as much
    As intelligent Mr. Toad!

The animals sat in the Ark and cried,
Their tears in torrents flowed.
Who was it said, "There's land ahead"?
Encouraging Mr. Toad!

The Army all saluted
    As they marched along the road.
Was it the King? Or Kitchener?
    No. It was Mr. Toad!

The Queen and her Ladies-in-waiting
    Sat at the window and sewed.
She cried, "Look! who's that *handsome* man?"
    They answered, "Mr. Toad."

Kenneth Grahame

THE WHALE

There was a most Monstrous Whale:
He had no Skin, he had no Tail.
When he tried to Spout, that Great Big Lubber,
The best he could do was Jiggle his Blubber.

Theodore Roethke

49

SEAL MOTHER'S SONG

Oh! hush thee, my baby, the night is behind us,
 And black are the waters that sparkled so green.
The moon, o'er the combers, looks downward to find us
 At rest in the hollows that rustle between.
Where billow meets billow, then soft be thy pillow;
 Ah, weary wee flipperling, curl at thy ease!
The storm shall not wake thee, nor shark overtake thee,
 Asleep in the arms of the slow-swinging seas.

Rudyard Kipling

FOUR FURRY SEALS, FOUR FUNNY FAT SEALS

Four furry seals, four funny fat seals
Ork! Ork! Ork!
With silly seal stunts for four fish meals
Ork! Ork! Ork!

Four furry seals blowing horns, toot toot
Ork! Ork! Ork!
Flapping their flippers in a seal salute
Ork! Ork! Ork!

Four furry seals bouncing big beach balls
Ork! Ork! Ork!
Croaking clamorous silly seal calls
Ork! Ork! Ork!

Four furry seals striking silly seal poses
Ork! Ork! Ork!
Balancing hoops on their silly seal noses
Ork! Ork! Ork!

Four furry seals, four funny fat seals
Ork! Ork! Ork!
With silly seal stunts for four fish meals
Ork! Ork! Ork!

Jack Prelutsky

THE PERSONABLE PORCUPINE

Now a young porcupine
Makes a passable pet,
Though he sneezes and snorts
If his prickles get wet.

So bathe him with caution
And dry him with care,
Shampoo well his whiskers
And massage his hair.

He's tender and loving,
A fair dinkum friend
Whose sweet disposition
I well recommend.

There's no need to sing him
Asleep of a night,
Just tell him a story
And tuck him in tight.

He'll scare away lap-dogs,
Cockroaches and rats,
And frighten the life out
Of unwary cats.

He likes pickled parsnips,
Baked bananas and bread;
But one word of warning —
Keep him out of your bed!

Wilbur G. Howcroft

SKUNK

Skunk's footfall plods padded
    But like the thunder-crash
He makes the night woods nervous
    And wears the lightning-flash —

From nose to tail a zigzag spark
    As warning to us all
That thunderbolts are very like
    The strokes he can let fall.

That cloudburst soak, that dazzling bang
    Of stink he can let drop
Over you like a cloak of tar
    Will bring you to a stop.

O Skunk! O King of Stinkards!
    Only the Moon knows
You are her prettiest, ugliest flower,
    Her blackest, whitest rose!

Ted Hughes

CAT BATH

She always tries
to look her best —
she washes east,
she washes west,
she washes north,
she washes south
with the washcloth
in her mouth.

And then, without
a sign of rush,
she makes her tongue
a comb and brush
to groom her fur
or, should she choose,
to smooth the velvet
of her shoes.

Aileen Fisher

SNICKETTY SNACKETTY SNEEZE

Snicketty snacketty sneeze.
A mouth is on the cheese
Giving the cheese a kiss.
A lucky thing it's Swiss.

Look out! That little gray mouth
Is running all over our houth!
It's trying to catch the cat!
Quick, fetch the baseball bat!

It's gone. It's heading south.
Micketty macketty mouth.

X. J. Kennedy

OLD HOGAN'S GOAT

Old Hogan's goat was feeling fine,
Ate six red shirts from off the line;
Old Hogan grabbed him by the back
And tied him to the railroad track.
Now when the train came into sight,
That goat grew pale and green with fright;
He heaved a sigh, as if in pain,
Coughed up those shirts and flagged the train!

American folk rhyme

THE ANSWERS

"When did the world begin and how?"
I asked a lamb, a goat, a cow:

"What's it all about and why?"
I asked a hog as he went by:

"Where will the whole thing end, and when?"
I asked a duck, a goose, a hen:

And I copied all the answers too,
A quack, a honk, an oink, a moo.

Robert Clairmont

RACCOON

The raccoon wears a black mask
And he washes everything
Before he eats it. If you
Give him a cube of sugar,
He'll wash it away and weep.
Some of life's sweetest pleasures
Can be enjoyed only if
You don't mind a little dirt.
Here a false face won't help you.

Kenneth Rexroth

THE HAPPY SHEEP

All through the night the happy sheep
Lie in the meadow grass asleep.

Their wool keeps out the frost and rain
Until the sun comes round again.

They have no buttons to undo,
Nor hair to brush like me and you,

And with the light they lift their heads
To find their breakfast on their beds

Or rise and walk about and eat
The carpet underneath their feet.

Wilfred Thorley

SHEEP

When sheep
Can't sleep
Do they make a big fuss,
Or do they just go ahead
And begin
To count
Us?

Mike Thaler

PETS

Once we had a little retriever
But it bit our beaver
Which had already bitten
Our Siamese kitten
Which had not been pleasant
To our golden pheasant.
The pheasant took a dislike to Laura,
Our Angora,
Who left her hairs
On the Louis Quinze chairs

And her paws
On one of our jackdaws
Who were not at all nice
To our white mice
Who were openly rude
To our bantam brood
Whose beaks were too sharp
For our golden carp
Who were on rotten terms
With our silk-worms

Who were swallowed up
By our retriever pup
Who consequently died
With all the silk inside.
Then we knew we'd have to buy
Something so high
And stout and strong it
Would let no body wrong it;
So we purchased a Hyena
Which, though it ate my sister Lena
And some embroidery off the shelf,
Remained intact itself
And has not yet died
So that our choice was justified.

Daniel Pettiward

THE RACCOON

The raccoon wears a mask at night
And has a brown-ringed tail.
That's how I recognize him when
He dumps my garbage pail.

Pyke Johnson, Jr.

THE TALE OF A DOG

When my little dog is happy,
    And canine life is bliss,
He always keeps his joyful tail

.
s
i
h
t
  e
   k
    i
A-standing up l

When my little dog is doleful,
    And bones are scarce, you know,
He always keeps his mournful tail
    A-hanging 'way d
                        o
                        w
                        n
                        l
                        o
                        w
                        .

James H. Lambert, Jr.

BIG BLACK DOG!

Mother says I'm not to go
    Past that house at night —
They have an awful big black dog
    And HE MIGHT BITE.

But my friend Jane
    Says that's not quite right,
She says she knows the dog
And he would NEVER BITE.

What shall I do?
    I think I'll go tonight,
I really must find out
    WHO IS RIGHT.

So I went and stared right at him
    I gave him such a fright
He looked as if he thought
    I MIGHT BITE!

Carol Michael

THE HOUSE OF THE MOUSE

The house of the mouse
is a wee little house,
a green little house in the grass,
which big clumsy folk
may hunt and may poke
and still never see as they pass
this sweet little, neat little,
wee little, green little,
cuddle-down hide-away
house in the grass.

Lucy Sprague Mitchell

"I AM HOME," SAID THE TURTLE

"I am home," said the turtle, as it pulled in its head
And its feet, and its tail. "I am home, and in bed.

"No matter what inches and inches I roam,
When the long day is done, I am always at home.

"I may go whole feet . . . even yards . . . in a day,
But I never get lost, for I'm never away

"From my snug little house and my snug little bed.
Try being a turtle! — That's using your head!

"You can go on forever, no matter how far,
And whatever you need is wherever you are!"

("Is there one thing I miss when I'm snuggled in tight?
Yes: there's no room for someone to kiss me good night.")

John Ciardi

THORNY

That briar patch looks uninhabitable;
In fact I doubt it's even rabbitable!

William Cole

THE MOUSE ATE THE BAIT

The mouse ate the bait off.
The trap didn't spring.
He didn't just nibble it,
He ate the whole thing,
Did a little mouse dance
Shivering with glee,
Used it for a bathroom
And waved his tail at me.

Mildred Luton

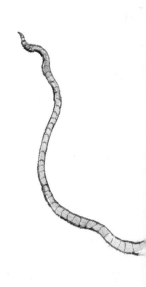

DIMPLETON THE SIMPLETON

Dimpleton the simpleton
    Went out to milk a cow.
Dimpleton the simpleton
    Could not remember how.

He pumped her tail, both high and low,
    To make the milk come out;
The cow went Moo, the bucket flew,
    And smacked him on the snout!

Dennis Lee

LIFE

I met four guinea hens today,
creaking like pulleys.

"A crrk," said one,
"a crrk," said two,
"a crrk," said three,
"a crrk," said four.

I agree with you cheerfully, ladies.

Alfred Kreymborg

GROUNDHOG DAY

In February when few gusty flakes
Above the frozen sheets of snow still hover,
Out of his hole the sleepy groundhog breaks
To peek around and see if winter's over.

Then if he finds his shadow, back he shies
To nap while deeper drifts the wind shall bring;
But if no shadow shows beneath dark skies
He waddles through the ditch to look for spring.

Marnie Pomeroy

ALWAYS BE KIND TO ANIMALS

Always be kind to animals,
Morning, noon, and night;
For animals have feelings too,
And furthermore, they bite.

John Gardner

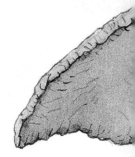

INDEX

ACKNOWLEDGMENTS

Every effort has been made to trace the ownership of all copyrighted material and to secure the necessary permissions to reprint these selections. In the event of any question arising as to the use of any material, the editor and the publisher, while expressing regret for any inadvertent error, will be happy to make the necessary correction in future printings.

Grateful acknowledgment is made to the following for permission to reprint the copyrighted material listed below:

Basil Blackwell Ltd. for "The Happy Sheep" by Wilfred Thorley.

William Cole for his poem "Thorny."

Geoffrey Dearmer for his poem "The Giraffe."

Doubleday for "The Bat," copyright 1938 by Theodore Roethke. "The Whale," copyright © 1961 by Theodore Roethke. From *The Collected Poems of Theodore Roethke* by Theodore Roethke. Used by permission of Doubleday, a division of Bantam Doubleday Dell Publishing Group, Inc.

HarperCollins Publishers for "About the Teeth of Sharks" by John Ciardi, from *You Read to Me, I'll Read to You*, by John Ciardi. © 1962 John Ciardi. "Cat Bath" by Aileen Fisher from *My Cat Has Eyes of Sapphire Blue* by Aileen Fisher. © 1973 by Aileen Fisher. Reprinted by permission of HarperCollins Publishing.

Houghton Mifflin Company for "I Am Home, Said the Turtle" from *Doodle Soup* by John Ciardi. Text copyright © 1985 by Myra J. Ciardi. Reprinted by permission of Houghton Mifflin Company. All rights reserved.

Wilbur G. Howcroft for his poem "The Personable Porcupine."

Pyke Johnson, Jr. for "The Toucan" by Pyke Johnson, Jr. © 1972 Pyke Johnson, Jr. for "The Raccoon" by Pyke Johnson, Jr.

X.J. Kennedy for "Snicketty Snacketty Sneeze" by X.J. Kennedy. By permission of the author. Copyright © 1992 by X.J. Kennedy.

Mildred Luton for her poem "The Mouse Ate the Bait."

Doug MacLeod for his poem "Anaconda."

Macmillan Publishing (reprinted with permission of) for "Four Furry Seals" from *Circus* by Jack Prelutsky. Copyright © 1974 by Jack Prelutsky. For "The Song of Mr. Toad" by Kenneth Grahame from *The Wind in the Willows* © 1961 Scribners.